Twang

Poems

Ben Kline

Copyright © 2025 Ben Kline

All rights reserved. No part of this publication may be reproduced, distributed, or transmitted in any form or by any means, including photocopying, recording, or other electronic or mechanical methods, without the prior written permission of the publisher, except in the case of brief quotations embodied in critical reviews and certain other noncommercial uses permitted by copyright laws. For permission requests, write to the publisher at the address below.

ELJ Editions Ltd. is committed to publishing works of quality and integrity. In that spirit, we are proud to offer this collection to our readers. This is a work of poetry. All views expressed within are Ben Kline's.

ISBN: 978-1-942004-99-8

Library of Congress Control Number: 2025935090

Cover Art: Jesse Kramer

ELJ Editions, Ltd.
P.O. Box 815
Washingtonville, NY 10992

www.elj-editions.com

Praise for *Twang*

Up close, it sounded like the men when they finished, their faith, jostling what they didn't understand against what they secretly wished, writes poet Ben Kline in his unflinching new book *Twang*, a must have collection that bristles with holler talk, hay fields, double-wides, Styrofoam coolers of beer, Satan, Madonna and the fervor of kissing boys and no name men by the lake. A place where *gay demons [bring] ruin to what upstanding citizens call decency*, though a $50 dollar donation to the church can go a long way in saving a soul from eternal damnation. Kline brings gristle, gut and bone, giving voice to what it means to grow up deeply rural, Appalachian and queer, busting open every stereotype along the way.

–Kari Gunter-Seymour, Ohio Poet Laureate, Author of *Dirt Songs*

With language lush as Whitman's and a cadence that twirls between Madonna and creation epics, Ben Kline's "Twang" breathes life into Appalachia in ways we have never witnessed before. Tender, bucolic, celestial, erotic, queer—Kline's poems are a tractor bucking, a lover's touch in the dark, witchcraft wrought from honey and river baptisms, uncles dissolving like the Eucharist. Brilliant and immense, "Twang" is a true literary feat. "Don't they know / my dirt tongue / sops the blood / off their faces?"

–Todd Dillard, author of *Ways We Vanish* and *Ragnarök at the Father-Daughter Dance*

Ben Kline strikes a miraculous balance between offering us individual poems that are honed—precise in their formal choices, deeply musical, tightly coiled—yet add up to a collection that has the wild architecture and unfurling sprawl of a novel. *Twang*'s complicated portrait of family dynamics, occasionally tender but often violent, and the blood and gristle of living close to the land, is matched by its nuance in capturing a very specific American political and economic era that is stitched-through by the realities of queerness in a time when the AIDS Quilt felt like a shout against the void. "After she caught me voguing Mom told the third cousins / I took drugs," confides the opening to "My Villain Origin Story," a playful title that, as is so often the case with Kline's humor, yields an unsparing truth. *Twang* isn't a book you read; *Twang* is a world you step into.

—Sandra Beasley, author of *Made to Explode*

The Poems

Augur 3
The New Math 4
Country Queer 6
Let Us Pray 9
Reading Is Fundamental 11
Cento for 1985 15
Hayfield Prayer 16
Silence = Death 17
B 18
First Cousins 20
A good lie is a winning bluff 21
Cottonmouth 23
Calliphora Vomitoria 24
Red Spots in the Snow 26
Plague 27
Symphony of the Holler 28
Bullies 30
August Aubade 32
Second Cousins 34
Farm Life Wasn't All Servitude and Trauma 35
Damned Spots 36
Will / Inherit 40
Common Source Minerals in the Bottom Tip of Ohio's Heart 41
Be a Good Boy 43
Redneck Arithmetic 44
Pawpaw 46
August Serenade 47

They Say Men Are Always About Looks 49
My Villain Origin Story 50
A Lisp 51
To August 52
Third Cousins 54
Flower Moon 55
Uncle Nick 56
Sawyer 59
Seizure 60
Part Time Jobs in Appalachia 62
Antidote 63
Fourth Cousins 65
Prosody, or an Origin Story 67
Oil & Ambivalence 69
Death = 71
Detente 72
Dead Young Uncles 74
August Gloria 75
Damn, I wish I was your lover 76
Dead Young Uncles 78
Strange Orange 81
Dress Nice and Smell Good 83
Whine 85
Glasnost 87
Twang 88
Holler Psalm 6:02 90
Always August 91

Notes 92
Acknowledgements 96
About the Author 98

Augur

Every summer, the field between our house and the creek cracked, zigzags wide enough to hide a copperhead or break an ankle. Not from drought, Dad said. Just August. Even in wet years when young corn crowded the fence, stalks would vanish at dusk, turn up in the winter plow. Like my older cousins, ripe with pit musk and cedar rub, who went to town Saturday *looking for tonight or a wife*. Who turned up Sunday, sliding into the last pew after the first reading.

In drought or fallow seasons, the field rolled too, baring its silt belly and old ash, an occasional femur. Dad said a fella could vanish in its soft spots. I crawled through thistles and iron weeds, patting the soil, digging holes by hand. I found dust and molts, seeds in starling shit. Not a single spot into which I could vanish like my uncle, deep into his fifth, mumbling about me not liking girls *the right way*. I kept digging, through orphan roots and detritus, germinating, ready.

The New Math

Every third Saturday
at the floodplain ball field,

deputies opened the gates,
trucks lined up, raising

dust or pushing mud,
tailgates dropped

to support big men
in tan overalls, faded

Reds ball caps
hiding haggling eyes.

Between displays of rifles
and shotguns, pistols,

the occasional grenade,
Grandpa told us things

like *trickle down
is some damned liar's math*

as he inspected bullets
arranged like the rainbow

of taffies he bought us
at the drugstore.

I twisted the pink
raspberry wrappers

one end at a time,
watched the older boys

still blind and bruised
by Friday night

stroke barrels and finger
triggers, knife blades, testing

the pressure, asking about the kick
like they didn't know the words

for how it made them feel
or if they should feel it. I knew.

Even when Grandpa said
It's a fool who shoots in public,

a random dad's rifle crack
scattering fog

and the hillside limestone
atop which I'd later meet

those boys in the woods
to practice bracing ourselves.

Country Queer

1
In the verdant low valley where the ancient Teays flowed & the glaciers crawled

home like a botched homicide, our farm was a caw's echo

west of the northbound Ohio whose magnetic sorcery

warded off good thoughts or new ideas

near the twenty barns dotting the farm. I hid in how many: three,

five? Never the same one twice. Punishment

was never my vice. Unlike men,

my aquifer of choices unwise.

2
From age five, I was part-time
with my father's LLC, but full-time
in the field, filing my first 1040A

at age ten. Reagan gave me no refund
which didn't make me great then, either.
I was skinny, my pine needle arms

able to enter breeched cows
writhing like greased sacks
we'd flatten on the barn floor

to protect new potatoes
or wobbly baby Charolais
rising shimmery pink.

I hated clipping neat red vees
in their diaphanous ears
every March, their banded scrotums

littering the barn lot like soccer balls
for the feral cats & I protested
the shiny elastrator

we used on the older calves,
its distinct crunch
abrupt as a funeral cough.

By eleven, I gave up
giving them names
like Skunk Tail & Pop Bottle,

Psychokick & Big Brahm.
Like any name, they faded
into the middle amber

of August's shrinking daylight.
Like my name, unused
by men who called me

       faggot.

3
Men with out of state plates
    like Kentucky Mud Blond

and Tennessee Dong—they saw it
    in my shallow end eyes as green

as moss atop my bedrock,
    my gaze lingering like blood loss

as I swallowed the dark waters
        of ditch, creek, pond, crack & cock

between six-day work weeks—
        seven if the sky stretched wide

& we recognized signs
        in the cumuli shapes

between milkings, cleaning stalls,
        stacking bales until Uncle Jay

backed over a tabby kitten—
        the dump truck had a sticky clutch

& the other cats gathered
        round their freshly dead friend,

their low frequency hymn
        mistaken for purring by city cousins.

Up close, it sounded like the men
        when they finished, their faith

jostling what they didn't understand
        against what they secretly wished.

The cats knew. Our terriers too,
        flinging snakes by the neck

because Satan likes it rough
        & Christians happily oblige

until caught cash in hand
        or cock in mouth

when the lights click on.

Let Us Pray

Our pile of cousins congregates at 8:30, stacks hickory and elm atop old
  Tribunes, oak leaves gasping for the match.

The first cousins bring beer and joints, plastic jugs of sour water to numb our
  tongues.

Above the pit and switchgrass, embers crack darkness. Coals stay up all night.

Pop, pretzels and chips, sleeping bags arrive with the second cousins. Ursa
  Major watches.

The thirds craft cover stories about the drive-in, collect cash for next time.

Every cousin brings their pocketknife.

I open mine
last, cleanse
the blade with spit

and flame. It glows,
a stick of sunset
cooling pink as inside

my lips. With the pile
circling the fire, I split
my ring finger's tip, blood

hissing between tongues
and smoke. The cut
flares. Did you know,

a third asks, that fire
is a chemical reaction
outside of any state of matter?

                                                      Yes, I do,

                              wavering between starlight
                                        and our ash.

Reading Is Fundamental

Lesson 1

What're we gonna do tonight? / Lotus-legged circle in Grandma's den / around a foot-high stack of newspapers to roll / *I say we drive down to Huntington* / giving good face around the room / the category best friends for Jon and Henri / guest starring cousin Pat and Wesley as Henri's boo / *and go to the Driftwood for drag / boys, ya turn me* / *Damn I love this song,* and then me / teetering off the bass rolling from Jon's new stereo / from a cassette tape by / a beautiful brown woman in white tee and snug faded jeans / *There's a lot for a Friday paper* / upside down round and round, instinctively / *Honey, people like sales* / Trickle down as a big move up to / any other side of town / respectively, as it were / *I say we go to the lake* / but I was from a farm, away / from the burn of / knowing, or not

Lesson 2

That reporter / dispatched from Tehran / *needs to shave* / where the claws of metal eagles failed to make fists / *Right? Bad news should come from* / saturated blues and greens on Grandma's new RCA / *good looking people* / But the former actor in the first commercial / *Can we watch something else?* / promised a great America again / *I mean, you know they'll kill them all* / not knowing the coming need for kindness / *Pat, can you reach the dial?* / More papers rolled, stacked pyramid / *Who the hell's buying shoes at K-Mart?* / Almost time for their bike route / *I dunno, honey. Your trailer cousins?* / Henri lifted an invisible teacup to his grin and winked / and Pat laughed, *Nah* / *my ma buys mine at Unger's* / and I wiggled my toes / squeezed into unbreathable plastic / brown Payless sneakers

Lesson 3

Guys, look. This was my uncle Reggie / Wesley unfolded a paper / Top left photo, a young black man halfway through / life at the bottom of the obits / *sad bits,* Grandpa always said / between sips after coming home from the mill / *Jeez, lotta dead people today, whole page worth* / Imagine dying without your name / no Jon, Henri, Wesley or Pat / just fledglings smashed flat from sudden impact, all flung / into the trash hole behind the horse barn / *Was really sorry to hear about him, Wes* / into flames angry enough to melt everything, even the boys / later left in trash bags by anxious orderlies passing the bill to hell / *Thanks, Pat, but truth, we weren't close* / after heaven refused to help / *They think he had cancer* / Imagine knowing without / words for your knowledge / *but I don't think they'll ever know for sure*

Lesson 4

Ok, let's wrap this up and get going / Pat finished his stack and mine, unknowingly rubbing / my arm aflame with a feeling he / *Folks need to get their news* / would articulate loudly a decade later / in a locked stall at the mall / *I still say we go to the Driftwood* / The papers stuffed into smudged eggshell canvas / bags slung over shoulders / *Hey everybody, having fun again?* / as they strutted toward the back-porch door / as Henri insisted the dress made / by someone named Mackie / *was fabulous, like a gown* / *woven with moonbeams and starlight* / and I wanted to / know how they have fun / go with them again / on the handlebars down 4th Street over / Grandma's objections and Jon's denials / when my mom found out / *I mean it matched her lashes!* / Henri and Wesley were demonstrating French / kissing for Pat the last time Jon / babysat me on Friday afternoon

Lesson 5

I can't believe she / halfway through a daydream about Spider-Man vs the Thing / *called us faggots* / Laughter opened the door / *She didn't call she yelled* / like an old piano finishing / with some jazzy ad libs / notes ahead of the melody as / bags crumpled on the kitchen floor / *That's because she doesn't know about Bobby* / joining the invisibility of wishes and prayers / *Or maybe she does* / Crosstalk cut the tar cloud / of Grandma's after-nap slims / like thwip thwips from web shooters trying / to stop Grimm from landing a kapow / *ugh who cares! Everyone has a secret. Sooooo,* / where it might actually hurt / *where are we going tonight?* / My mom would be back soon / taking me home with the groceries and pizza, four / loaves of bland wonder / for the deep freezer

Lesson 6

Can we please go back / upstairs in Jon's room, thigh to thigh with Pat on the lower bunk / *to that dress?* / Jon closed the door as Henri / adjusted boombox dials, / *Because it was everything and the leftovers* / restarting the cassette / *Is that Miss Ross?* / my small crooked finger turning their heads to / the poster of the giant black lady on / the back of the door *She seems* / *shiny like that Mackie* / and their laughter smothered the beat and the bass as Jon / took me by the wrists and spun me to dizzy / *That's Grace lil man, Grace Jones, a whole* / *different kind of goddess* / the boys a blur and I wanted to know / *Is she fabulous too?* / but my *fab* wobbled loose, flopping / off my lips, my maw not ready / for such girth / *Honey, she is* / *fierce!* and she resembled Storm right before she summons lightning to blow up Sentinels

Lesson 7

I think she looks like a superhero / Wesley gives me a second spin, higher / and faster, lacking the safety of being kin, thus / *She kinda does* / possessing a thrill unknown / *so like the complete opposite of most people round here* / People who might envy the freedom in this room / *You'll figure it out when you're older* / so small so safe / *Or he won't because he's...not?* / but I was / wanted to be / could not imagine / being any other way / *Should we be teaching him how to read?* / I could already read the newspaper. (Wesley Carter II, 43, died / at the King's Daughter Hospital on....) / Faces too, but / I took most note of names, / *Is it ever too early?* / especially after they're gone / *Have you seen him arch his eyebrow?* / and my nights grew too long, the crickets / harmonious *mmhmms* floating above / an unheard syncopated chorus of triple snaps

Cento for 1985

You're listening to 85.5 WFLD in a small town, where everyone
knows your family name at church, picnics, the five-and-dime

where Mr. McFee asks me about those concentric hexagons
I drive in the new cornfield and the pickup truck strangers give it

one more night, make the most of the dark and red dawn, taking
their broken wings to learn what happens head over heels. The tractor

never surrenders to dry clods, killdeer eggs, someone who cares
where we go, what we do, taking me with him to build the city

every time he goes away not wanting to rule the world the way
my father shouts, letting my mother's silence out. Take me on,

beyond these hills. You've tuned in to 85.5, all the hits, the disc
pulverizing the silt on which I can't dance for inspiration. Would I

lie to you? Careless whispers are when you love somebody and things
can only get better. Hexagons become rectangles. Easy lovers

hold on, growing pains my knees, but how will I know if I belong
to the city, the night, lizard tongued men eating rats, a dynasty

or a friend back again, a party of new confidantes? I slow it down,
use my gum to plug a hydraulic leak, not needing another hero who

could show me back to the future brimming with boys of summer
walking sunshine alive, kicking down the fortress around my heart.

Hayfield Prayer

Grinding between third and fourth, the tractor dry heaved. I said *y'uns* instead of y'all, Dad shouting from the hay wagon, invoking God and the flat *tar*, the groundhog hole I didn't clear, rain threatening to ruin the alfalfa he'd rolled into rows for the baler. Dad's trash pit plumed charcoal over us and the narrow holler field. Sparrows and starlings circled, only crows went through. They know, Dad said. The pit's *far* could handle cherubs weeping. It burned for days, its small star swaddled in silica and fertilizer bags. I could handle the switch cut from the *crick* maple with Dad's pocketknife, leaves stripped by his calloused hand. I thought of seraphim as he approached, and the tractor died.

Silence = Death

Peter Jennings broke into the Pepsi commercial—
Rock Hudson dead at 59. From AIDS. The graphic
footage of his sunken face wobbling
through a recent segment with Doris Day.
My city Grandma gasped. I didn't—
I knew about Rock Hudson already.
Grandma and I spent afternoons
watching *Pillow Talk* instead of *Looney Tunes*.
For ninety minutes, she neglected cigarettes
and I breathed loose and free, clapping along
to the theme song, lobbing the blue
sofa pillows across the coffee table
as we kicked our legs in the air.
I always opened another butterscotch
while mouthing "talk about the boy
I'm gonna marry someday." We swooned
when Rock lifted his leg above the bubbles,
but only I knew why his grin curled that way,
what lurked in the long pauses
wedged between the disappointments
his characters uttered. Grandma often
dozed off during "You Lied," waking
for the tidy ending that ignored
his fluttered upgaze, his debonair
swoop I mimicked around my aunts, uncles
who squinted when I spoke too fast
with my hands. I knew,
but I didn't want to
change my name or lie
about having a strange cancer
in Paris. I didn't want to
die young, ahead of Grandma
turning to me, her tears
from a future I knew
could be mine.

B

Grandpa had an S for his middle name.
No period, just my S

sliding out his pink mouth like a kazoo
summoning copperhead revenants.

He fortified his sweet tea with honey, brown
pours from his flask, his theory

about mud daubers being honeybees cast
in purgatory, forced to live

in the dirt. *They never land on dandelions.*
He pointed at the yard, sunny

white florets abuzz with harvest, bumbles
and hornets bobbing trajectories.

I wanted to snatch one by the wings, ask
about their dauber cousins

whose queens order the capture of crab
and yellow spiders for the larder,

and I wanted to slice my first name
from my last with my B

like a sting when it breaks the skin.
I'm not sure how they fit

in those little pipes. Grandpa knocked one
loose from the porch corner

with his steady stick. Crumbs bounced, broke
into dust, larvae and black

eyeballs rolling into the grass, pedipalp
ghosts on the breeze.

And they're so quiet. Were I as scorned,
my sting so fraught,

I would be too.

First Cousins

after Whitman

We unveiled our pale cocks, larvae bobbing under the pond's green-shine, lunch for snapping turtles.

We flexed our throats, laughter past hayfields and football, our jocund warble rustling cattails at the deep end.

A few had thickened, swirling black hairs the rest of us marveled around the tractor tire tube.

What was the world, our quiet valley of hay and oaks, if our bodies could so quickly become their own and we could see it.

There was no one to see us.

There was no one to hear us, scold us, no one to protest the loose angles of my wrists and hips.

I lowered my waistband and kicked my feet, treading inches away.

I lowered myself into muck, the slither of my cottonmouth permitted to engirth what could corrupt me, and I refused to balk.

I refused the feeling of a hand. The feeling was not my innocence.

It was my curious symphony, seeking a finale, wonderful vigor glimpsed across a man's back sun-kissed in a film or magazine, kissed to end the story, promising health, longevity.

There was no one to tell us, but our cocks knew. They always knew.

A good lie is a winning bluff

my sister said, her ankle
blooming taut fuchsia

and cumulus blue, loose bits
crunching when she drew

a circle above her head
with her toes, the air

rhythmic with our brother's whimper,
my laugh cracking too.

How did this happen
I could hear Mom asking,

but Sis leapt like a frog
from a pond lightning

lit up, saying yes
before I finished the dare,

flinging herself down
to a thud, her ankle wrong

in dry dung. Our brothers
ran to tattle. *How did this*

even happen? Dad swung
his belt. Mom made a bag

of ice. Brother grinned
like a win, but I didn't blink.

Not then or years later
when Sis couldn't explain

she'd been with another girl
the night she snuck out

the half-bath window, a paper
clip in the latch as I'd shown her.

Cottonmouth

New and crisp save the corner he'd singe,
Dad hid five-dollar bills throughout our house—
slipped between thawed slices of bread, folded
quadruple in the candy bowl, in the leather-bound volume
of Shakespeare's complete works on my desk—
most of *Coriolanus* hollowed out to hide
my rubbers and phone numbers, the note
in which my uncle warned me
about looking strange older men in the eye.
Dad made us look him in the eye,
wanted my brothers and me on the straight
and narrow side of the family, thwarting
my curve into vice after a cousin nun
taught me to count deals on a chrome lighter—
not a sin, she said, just a strategy like Reagan's *Star Wars*
or leading with the right bower. I usually left
the money where I found it—
shifting it to the next sonnet, under corn flakes
instead of raisin bran, in my brother's coat pocket.
Dad wrapped his belt around our thighs
if he caught us with cash Mom didn't dispense,
even the eight ones I exchanged from her business drawer
for two fives I thought he'd forgotten. Unlike
the scar his buckle's prong left on my ass—
all for some X-Men comics, the new Madonna,
more rubbers and videotape head cleaner,
my mortal coil like a cottonmouth
lurking at the gush end of a culvert, watching for mice
swept loose when a downpour flooded the barn.

Calliphora Vomitoria

I arranged the femurs in a heptagon

like Aunt Pat taught us between *TV Guide*

and afterschool chardonnays. I made sure

to shine the epiphyses before binding each

with Juicy Fruit, before the preacher

buying alfalfa from us side-eyed me & my dirt-

covered red vestments borrowed from the sacristy—

we were Catholic farmers in a Baptist sea

of miners' wives and horsemen rolled holier than

this rot curse requiring bones of dogs not our own,

their marrow two seasons in the sun.

Anything buried is just dead,

ghoulish as mid-Mass flatulence, the steeple

of caudal vertebrae wobbling as I added

sweet ligaments from my mouth, the wrappers

piled for the fire, a name written inside each one.

Aunt Pat warned us to spell them right or we'd have

to chew at least a hundred four-leaf clovers

to cud our soured guts. I squeezed

my little blue ballpoint. I didn't know

the preacher's first name, only his oldest son's,

the youngest too—they insisted

I repeat them, their dirty fingers

around my face after my gaze gave me away

and we ended up in the loft, and I made

no mistakes of letter or bone, my seven-sided blaze

dancing as they tossed bales onto their flatbed,

the oldest unknotting ropes, coughing–

a loud blue fly rushed into his mouth.

Red Spots in the Snow

Uncle, you kept leaving me as if I were that boy Jimmy who lived up Jenkins Holler with his mom and four older brothers in a flaking blue shotgun house with no screen door and a dirt yard. Skinny, light brown Jimmy who never said his last name, who fed his five shepherd mutts before himself, who slumped in the front seat of the bus, blinking his big brown eyes at the floor before and after he ate his neon green shoestrings for junior high bullies. That Jimmy, who deputies later found a week before fifth grade, his ears tucked in his left sneaker, his big toes in the other, and they had to pry his right thumb from the lighter receptacle of that white jeep left idling to empty between riverside dunes of culm. They found his newly asymmetric head shaved and shoved under the brake pad, his left eye dangling from the rear view by blue veins tied in a bonnet knot, and even then you vanished inside the hillside shed that smelled too clean to have a tar roof, reappearing Sunday mornings to snarl down pew when I would not sit still, because I stayed busy chasing clues about where the killers hid the rest of Jimmy, why the sheriff never arrested anyone when we all knew about the trail of red spots in the snow. I stayed busy with all the other shiny curiosities carried by the murder to the government woods above the limestone cliffs that remembered the river before us, white-eyed crows watching from branches in the leafless walnut tree that loomed like a twelve-armed ghost at the pullover, heads titled as if they might bring me splints for my dislocated fingers or shake their shiny black remiges to make room for my original teeth, which you kept leaving on the floor, leaving me a little bloody and smirking through raw gaps, leaving my tongue to hiss and spit and lisp when you growled like a dull saw.

Plague

In his paisley handkerchief tied to his walking stick like a windsock
Grandpa caught cicadas. Most, he beheaded
and dipped in chocolate syrup
he *fixed up* with his flask,
chewing until he spit their legs out,

but one, he held close to my face, its persimmon eyes looking back,
wings tympanic on his fingers, on its mission
to cover every oak and eat every leaf,
to croon all day and night, making love
before another seventeen years of sleep.

Imagine being so insistent and momentarily eternal,
though I knew from the 1986 World Book they laid eggs
and died, hatched nymphs tunneling dirt until heaven called.
Like me, they knew silence equals death,
the same fervor of kissing another boy again

after last night's dance. I wanted
their patience, and when Grandpa released the bug
I returned to dissecting a groundhog in the yard,
Grandpa repeating *esophagus, adrenal,*
duodenum around his toothpick,

asking if every cecum glowed. I flipped my knife
and sliced the sac, freeing dozens of eyes and legs
yellow with xylem sap and bile. Imagine
being so doomed and simultaneously
resilient.

Symphony of the Holler

I enter the pinewood

where the limestone breach
    begins the narrow

ditch and the crickets bow in, low

adagio at first, just a few, young males
    from their pitch and tempo

beckoning. *Find us, climb through
    the dark*, as if

my hands could answer

like presto, with duration, an attempt to scale
    falling off

because I cannot see.

I am the quiet part

of the movement. Call me a caesura, but play me
    backward and I might

go home. The crickets scrape

their tegmina, up and down, eager teeth

to please potential lovers, wanderers
    like me, my ā

flat on my tongue, held down by thumbs

that forbid me to speak at home. I play
    by hand, slowly
        at first.

The shortleaf brush my bare arms, find my back
    a dream they'd forgotten

they enjoy, crickets enjoining frogs

in the marsh below, an owl waiting
    for a sleepless chipmunk,

every moment a precipice

I cannot cross

until I do, my ā to crescendo, rounding
    the loblollies,
        my plops

tinkling the briar and brush floor, notes

too short to count

as rondo. I'm run out
    by coyotes

gathering farther up the hill, yipping

for my spilled scent, my last movement
    a death
    so small

it segues to the crickets
    dimming, the moon

walking me out of the grove,
    down the hill

past the barn bubbling with the gossip of bats.

Bullies

Do fifty push-ups. Saunter
like your uncle showed you
to the sunbathing garter's tail.

Grab it—enthrall the city
kids, girlfriends, the bullies
throwing rocks at the goats.

Shake it to confusion, dodging
bite—an absence of venom
lessens no pain. Twirl it

until it's a corkscrew ribbon
and someone says *Oooo*.
Take a deep breath. Wipe

any sweat on your jeans—never
try it in shorts or a swimsuit.
Crack it like a wet whip,

snapping between your knees—
a loose flick yanked into your chest.
Someone will always yell *Oh shit*

and at least two people will puke
when the snake's head pops
clean off its glottis—

unblinking eyes scatter
like marbles the nearby cats
kick around until the football players

return to the bus. Toss the carcass
in the weeds. Sit in the seat
behind the driver, under her mirror,

where she can't see you slipping
tips down your pants, dodging
the beating you took last time.

August Aubade

First beams spread through the haze
last night never lifted, surprising young grapes
and black-eyed Susan, suddenly tall
verdant west county senior running backs
so often shirtless, appearing malnourished
if corn-fed and resilient. Holler boys who ride
the bus ninety minutes for two-a-day scrimmages,
who huddle and perspire and shout playbook Morse,
helmets clanging against concussions, keeping time
like a redneck hi-hat right before fall semester,
new homerooms and names to scribble in the margins,
the varsity squad in new white tights, quiz bowl practice
a hive of answers I find in dictionaries and newspapers.
My street knowledge only covers reversing a breach birth
in a second-year heifer without showering in her broken water,
punching with the base of your palm like a ninja,
never selling black mollies to drunk college kids,
telling that east river junior to slide his tongue
a little deeper, unlike the bottle gentians
refusing the honeybees' advances. Those boys
chug soft drinks from gallon jugs, call out nicknames
revised from the previous years when I too
was a dandelion not yet to seed, spreading too easily
when that tall blond Freewill Baptist hurdler
leapt up the bus steps, grinning while squeezing in
against me, our bare arms and denim thighs
convecting temperatures without known unit,
despite my research into plasma, because we are not
those ions adrift in dark matter, not yet,
despite the warming troposphere between us
and the sun sinking into a lower arc over the valley,
drying the second cutting alfalfa just a little more slowly,

coaxing the sneezeweed into bloom, their toothy
yellow petals grazing my hips, tipping me off
to what might soon confuse me,
what might later undo me
and the other boys wiping their faces
on their already-soaked shirt fronts.

Second Cousins

Two boys from our town branch
    slipped under in the preacher's grip,
        holding what he told us about bones

in the pond muck, holding back tears
    their fathers would belt dry. He held them,
        repeating their names until they gargled

back to life, *praise be*, red mud
    gushing out their noses. Everyone
        on the shore clapped. *Praise be.*

I kept my switchblade quiet,
    eyes wide in the murk, his viper
        splitting the ripples, sawgrass, our zippers

and cheap cigarettes by the quarry.
    Like danger I wanted to be believed,
        to skinny dip, see the preacher

had changed, though I knew
    he hadn't. Everyone watching
        had my last name, knew the same

dead too. I knew we were bones,
    praise be. If anyone parted the water,
        would they see what happened to us?

Farm Life Wasn't All Servitude and Trauma

Three hours after Mass, one after pancakes
and bacon had settled, two dozen cousins
lined the gravel shore of the reservoir
slash swimming hole to find out who could flip
a full flip, then two, who could splash
Mom on the grassy shore without snagging
the line of her rod or knocking the can
of crawlers in her lap. Gary tried
a double lutz, landed in a split,
his howl called back by the cattle
in the lot. Dad gave him ice
from the cooler, I cracked a Dew,
dark blue cumuli bubbling the horizon,
a timer on our good time, this Sunday
free of sin and switchblades, loud
holler talk confusing the swallows
swooping to eat mosquitos dumb
with heat and hunger. Uncle Jay halfway'd
his somersault, his face and chest red
when he surfaced, our laughter a hymnal
inside the first rumble rolling east.
Dad gave us a thirty-minute warning,
I finished my pop, the dive line
a puppy's tail of hurry, climb up, jump,
yeehaws and more laughter, oh God,
joy I wish I could've bottled
like a firefly held to my face
nights I could only think of
my escape.

Damned Spots

                                    I.
I'm sweating out a paper about Lady Macbeth.
Mom enters, pulls off my headphones—
                              Your uncle Jon has AIDS
                              and he›s going to die.
Very *read my lips, no new taxes,*
but it feels like home—shotguns always
loaded under the seat, cousins told
what to say to deputies, Mom saying
my uncle, not her baby brother,
locking her bedroom door before nine.

I'm turning pages, remixing "Express Yourself"
choreography with A. C. Bradley citations—
my thesis navigates the queen as another weird sister
advocating unwise choices.

                                  II.
Midnight relaxes into ruin, hurly-burly and poppers.
George Michael in my ears—*Sometimes love can be mistaken*
for a crime—I'm under my sheet, filling a sock
while everyone else sleeps, knowing

I'm knuckled out of heaven
because like Jon, I can't keep it
to myself. I can't stay too full of milk
without ambition for more—
                              Mom never lets me
                              leave the farm too long—

more golden rounds of skinny dippers leaving the lake
at sunset, a tin of mints
chastising my tongue's curl
toward crack remarks—

I'm saying Lady Macbeth's a queer totem—
someone special, someone sacred—
in my conclusion, ambition for more
than *Jon's going to die?*

>Did his lovers understand
>or make themselves air?
>Did he/they do enough?

>III.

My paper earns an A—
Ms. Fisher floats a red question mark
over *Dame Judi Dench*, compliments
my framing of the queen as a diva fevered
with her failure to go solo.

>I want to solo
>where no one knows—

A letter from Jon arrives, says he's fine,
fever and nausea passing.

>Mom hasn't left her room.

I'm still thinking about the knives—

>how she took the time
>to smear the blood
>over their faces—

raising the stakes without planning
the consequences, the folly
of being too sure—

>I want to knock on the door.

                              I want to call my uncle.
                              I want to write a dozen short replies,
                              my paper enclosed—Are we more
                                            than our mistakes?

I rip them up, ride my bike past the rest area
to the lake, the rock shelter
he once warned me—

                              IV.

I'm burning ladybug wings
and pubic curls over squirrel

tail in a boulder's pock behind
the old coal furnace, a twig

added to the fire for every fool
who wishes villainy on any queen—

> Day and night o wicked deed
>   With many names I here seed
>
> Falwell weeping at Helms knees
>   Wildmon covered in Phelps fleas
>
> May Swaggert help you masturbate
>   May Roy Cohn meet you at Hell's gate
>
> Pray to Reagan, pray to Fate
>   In the lake wood, for love's sake

The smoke draws men from murky oak shade.
I see how they see me—treachery youth commits,

donning a new face every year. Their journey is thick—
loneliness trying to fancy itself—they want to kiss

my thighs, raze their truth without meeting my eye,
held together until the billows unfurl.

                        Mom leaves
her room to go to town for groceries—

the men leave, home to wives and deaf pillows,
their done deeds undone.
                      Don't they know
                      my dirt tongue

                      sops the blood
                      off their faces?

                      V.

Trouble wrings its hands in thunder
at our Memorial Day picnic—damned spots
climbing Jon's neck—feeling like home—
unwashed by the downpour—taking us
to the basement, to the kingdom come,
to patchouli spritzed on the cassette case
he hands me—I turn it over, the scent
inside Madonna's bejeweled navel
a dream of me standing alone
in the pines—those men
and queens calling
my name, holding Jon's arm
in the rain—the lesions
say he picked up the knives, yes,
slid them inside, his mouth open wide—
everyone must stand alone
and this perfume can't sweeten
the poison in his blood—
I wonder how it tastes—
a pansy stain in royal shades,
a crown I don't want to wear.

Will / Inherit

Suddenly / late summer / shirtless in the loft / he watches me / surmount the top rung / Stacked timothy exhaling June / The twine breaks / spreading soft blue / purple florets on which we lie / about men / the Virgin / glistening skin / senators and welfare / other things we cannot carry / like pistols / plastic bags / creek mud when it floods / uncovering July's empty cans / our fathers' distal bits / shredded mineral deeds / gold watches and fillings / silver rings my nephews will inherit / because we will leave / behind nothing

Be a Good Boy

Mom says *We're going at 2*. I'm in the basement, wearing a white tee and long johns, chopping sycamore, drinking High Life from the summer fridge, two cans, four. They didn't smash as easily then. Glow of the stove like penance. Or persuasion. Promises are just threats made nicely. I shower before we leave. *Only whores sweat in church*. I still did it for free. Before textbooks, rent and $4 gasoline. The Bushes didn't care about me then either. Click, pop, zzzzz, one more can, the best way to experience time. Now as always, same as that look Mom gives when I sigh. Tomorrow as yesterday when I lift that *Hustler* at the drugstore for the senior bullies who meet me behind the weight room, learning they might like doing more than viewing. 6th can's a blink. I feel for Father McKenzie. For all he knows about me, yet he smiles every Sunday at his magic show. The chalice never sparkles. The wafers still taste like paper. *You have to believe*. But what are the ingredients? How much cornstarch and yeast do you need to float on a holy breeze? I want to see. *It's been one month since* I realized death is blindness and echo. I want to see before I can't *in that time, I've committed several very mortal sins.*

Common Source Minerals in the Bottom Tip of Ohio's Heart

1. a) Black ribbon uncle's cash-coal . . . . Diamond future
   b) Elder fern, aflame . . . . Frozen creek

2. a) Bare limestone rods-mauve . . . . To touch, to ponder, to gaze
   b) Slip in the shale vein-blue . . . . Sleep demon, sleep
   c) Limestone cave of cocks-hollow . . . . Stalactite tears[3]

3. a) Crack in the shale-leak, come through . . . . Rinse off the dirt (Show me)
   b) Roadblock-granite (piece of who) . . . . Break his bones for free

4. a) Muddy rush-clay does not stay . . . . Take his bones to the creek[4]
   b) Vesuvius basin-limestone, grey . . . . Deeper than bones can see[5]

5. a) Sulphur Lake-algae glow . . . . Nairs you on full moons
   b) Black Lick-gravel, invisible turns . . . . The sycamores never tell
   c) McKenzie Point-feldspar, beer bottle shards . . . Drop your rod, your children and wives

---

1. Own the hilltop / Blow it off / Dynamite & air rights / Granpappy Calhoun gives it to you / Can you see it through?
2. Pray the Bradshaws never chamber / bullets to chance the ice / crossing where the barges / rut and die.
3. seen from my knees / caught by / wide eyes / licked to live / cleansed / I rise
4. The flow forgets us. / No sheriff finds us.
5. sunken cemetery / bookmarks of former lovers / fingertips following their faded names

6. a) Step & a Half-heart stone . . . . .Hurts the same, knows all their names[6]
   b) Frank Frank-red brick, thrown . . . . Strikes, breaks, asks no names
   (Go west, young man.)
   (Be safe)
   c) Men without names-boulders, sediment . . . . . Data incomplete (Insufficient)

7. a) Flood-sediment, bones grey . . . . .Who was no longer
   b) Calhoun, M-limestone, white . . . . A curse, a cause[7], dead cats[8]
   c) Smooth pebbles-limestone, quartz . . . . .Held, rubbed[9], wished

---

6. Johnson, Cox / Jenkins, Calhoun / Smith, Bradshaw / black book, left hook / everyone knows who knew
7. Pamphlets & newsletters / plain white envelopes / no return address
8. Heads clipped to the clothesline by their ears / Heads filled with irrational demographic fears
9. Some nights, / touch / is enough.

Redneck Arithmetic

Swill 5 shots of Wild Turkey
when dusk forgets
the cooling magenta
of midwinter afternoon
x
4 nights w/out reportable sleep
7 hours & 93 days after you stopped
seeking/seeing him
& his gold band
at (the birches crowding)
the fishing hole
÷
your uncle Joe's oak-handled axe
from the locked fence shed
→ firmly held w/ both hands
x
fingers forming a church roof
squirming like curtain-free confession
(cloudy beads condensing on the brow beams)
& Father T drops his Bible
twice (you told the truth!)
→ hammer forward
& both your arms bent
at 45°.
↓
Lock the door.
Close your eyes. Pour
what ounces remain of the 5th
through the cherry boards.
(Roaches drunk
in the dirt.)
+

Inhale & fall
forward (fall toward)

=

No epiphany, no envy
→ just hot sticky
swoon

+

teeth, bouncing
(into epitaph, Uncle,
at last.)

Pawpaw

On Dad's side of the family oak, every boy above twelve knew about the pawpaw, their church purple flowers and nether scent, their big bad seeds. Aunt Martie Renee would bake bread with them, add too many raisins, then peel and salt a bowlful for scooping at Granny's Decoration Day picnic. Granny called it Grave Day. *All the men I know are underground for this damned country*, she'd say. *All of 'em no good anyway.*

Marti Renee watched whose nose twitched above the pudding, who shifted in the hips. She sent shifty boys to the holler where the men were shooting bottles and beech trees. Where Uncle John C warned us about the toxins. How even a few seeds could rot your guts and limp your dick. *The skin too*, he'd say. *You gotta open it and git in the mushy part.* He flopped his lumpy tongue inside his cupped palm.

I knew what he was really talking about. A shifty boy was no good too, my tongue newly forked, combing bushes, ready to seed. Every day, grave.

August Serenade

Tangerine moon rises late, an only child
over those malachite end zones

flooded by lights too bright to be celestial,
breaking dusk under which I conceal

modern sentiments about chestnut manes
of wilting cornsilk, left nods at halftime

catalyzing instructions for assignments
performed behind the women's restrooms,

Heather squeezing out the stall window
into a split after a pyramid leap, sweat

salting her lips, slicking her thighs,
her pom-poms dropped by my knees

on the grass, as we planned last week
in chemistry, giggling through another

experiment in biomechanical reactions.
She shudders like a stiff aurous stalk

in the combine's maw, stripped then
conveyed to the wire crib to dry,

the sun retreating into shorter days
of less anxious languor, days that shrivel

like tomatoes too long on the post,
subjected to bugs, rejected by farmers.

After the game, at home drafting couplets,
pausing for illicit pours of iced PBR

to numb bites that might build character
were I quiet enough to be so Pentecostal,

I hear the fields sway in the glow, sharp
blades swooshing like snare drums

brushed for a twisted beat. Sleep
alchemizes memory into nostalgia

for sticky evenings, unproven hypotheses,
the cursive axioms of bats from the barn

eating bloated mosquitos while I note
other symmetries possible by rhyme.

They Say Men Are Always About Looks

but I fell in love over the phone
in 1990, his name two low notes

shoved out my throat, repeated
like a gulf smacking shore rocks

in starlight, our letters tucked
between issues of *Uncanny X-men*

because I did not want a willow
switch across my back,

did not want his hands cut off
before he could touch me.

When he called collect
on Sundays at 1:45, after Maghrib,

his parents asleep in their room,
he whispered *Do you ride the 3-wheeler*

alone? Do you name the baby cows?
Do you wear bib overalls without a shirt?

What is it like to bale hay? Yes, yes
and yes, hot and dirty, I said before

explaining Rogue's mutation, a touch
that removes, a safety in distance.

My Villain Origin Story

After she caught me voguing Mom told the third cousins
I took drugs. Never any specific class or high. Just drugs

whispered down the hallway, on the phone, in the vestibule
before Mass, I told a second cousin I was a witch. Not

a warlock or wizard, a witch, a queering they found confusing
until I flicked my tongue across the paten, told them God

tastes like cum, that a witch would know the Devil said so.
They gasped and clutched and told their parents, forcing

Mom to unwrap her lie, but they couldn't untangle me,
a skinny boy, being a witch. How can you be a witch?

You're a dude! But I was a witch in my tight jeans and white
tees, a skinny wannabe gender outlaw tangling my arms

to a beat Mom couldn't defeat, forced to tell the aunts
I might handle serpents, clutching my crotch, gasping

in my sleep about Peter and Michael holy inside me.
When I lifted the chalice, shouted *Body by wine*, the cousin

said I wasn't a witch or a wizard, just a nut who needed
a million Hail Marys and a beat down. Back home I rubbed

my nose to red in the hallway, whispering about blow and good
face, about Bette, Katherine, Lana too, my hips in a mood,

my wrists loose with sweat and crushed Excedrin Mom took
for no specific ailment I could look up or ask cousins about.

A Lisp

The priest said *any boy with a lisp has forsaken God.* He cupped an ear with his hand. *Listen for the devil's breath sliding through the fork of his tongue.* I nodded like several nearby uncles, turned my missal to the Sanctus. I'd kept my tongue against my teeth for years. *Hold them by the neck and press your thumbs into their unripe apple.*

He never explained why God would abandon anyone. Or why it was the devil's breath. When I asked my aunt Marie, she leaned on her hoe, shifted her wide brim, as if she might see the answer falling. *The good Lord tries his best, hon. Some sinners just enjoy the ruin too much.* I knew it wasn't ruin. When the salt stings it means you're still alive.

To August

> 1

> Iraq invaded Kuwait
> and we road-tripped east,

> our maroon '86 Caprice wagon
> with a backward backseat stopping

> at too many tchotchke shops, look-alike
> views along the Skyline Drive, gas suddenly

> a buck ten, voguing way mainstream and still
> too queer for the cousins at Sunday pasture baseball.

We didn't have cable on the farm, didn't lust for Arthur Kent
as the first Bush burned through Cheney's problems with uranium

> munitions, PATRIOT missiles, first-generation active denial systems
melting Baathists and Fighting Tigers alike, their mummies littering the desert.

Saddam didn't see it coming. Neither did those Tigers I joined at the park &
ride days before they deployed, staining our shirts with cum, my back with tears.

> 2

Cataract light gauzes contracting days,
    a ruse crickets chorus under potted mums,
        cracked clay, Styrofoam coolers of beer cans

emptied, crushed and forgotten, my freedom
    returns by early rise and bus rides, homework before
        hayfield, the barn looming liminal when the quarterback

brays to finish, flinging spit, musk potent as pills pulverized
    for snorting. He gives in my mouth. He gives no excuse.
        O teachers, withered with another August, invite me

into your rooms, assign my seat and hours of reading
    to escape granary labor I didn't seek, too meek to inherit
        our family land or the impatient looks of men

            leaking desire
            all over their fears.

3

Where are the stars? Cloaked by the petroleum plumes, fondling twilight in the pines, and my fingers prospect for roots to chew, earth fat to guzzle, any evidence they left behind, and find a worm yanked in two pinks thrashing to continue. The first coils my ring finger, the second disappears in fescue felled by machetes and hooves. I spit on the ring, and it tightens. My hunger burns behind my ribs. Where are they? Above the canopy thinning with each quickened dusk, they arrive later and later, fading in the blue bend around us, left to wander more mouths, my muddy hands cooling every pink to pale when we cheer a touchdown or missile strike, an empty can, problems we've solved.

Third Cousins

Orion loomed the twilight ledge, Rita and Mary sipping cans of beer in matching tan coveralls. *Don't think you should* – Rita opened her plastic bag and inhaled – *even consider it.* Mary poked the fire with her boot. *Not in New York City.* I cut the rolling papers too long to mess with Mary, to stretch the evening into night. *Why is it called house music anyway?* Our joints flared, tired stars caught between fingertips. *Sounds like robots made it.* Extra paper into the fire – *and I can't move that fast anymore* – whooshing to plasma before touching a flame, embers twirling across the blurry updraft. *Nothing worse than trying to be fancy when you don't know what is.* But I wanted to wake on their lumpy sofa and sprint home under pink yawn. To have muscular calves and a degree in physics, hair past my ears, – *Skinny B, you listening?* – men touching my curls and bare back at Rawhide. Men who wouldn't know my name or how to find me the next day. *Coz we don't want you to end up in the dirt.* More beautiful things than me came from the same dirt, and I wanted to find them.

Flower Moon

Debating Grandpa about which moon is best
for planting sweet corn and taters—
an early Flower Moon of course—
may not be as interesting as Mapplethorpe
scandalizing Cincinnati, every *Tribune* article
a warning about taxpayer waste and *gay demons*
bringing ruin to what upstanding citizens call decency,
said citizens being Falwells, Helms & Buchanans
swearing every soul saved will reconvene
under God's bright smile, a heavenly mission
to which you can donate fifty dollars today
and save a sinner from eternity's dense nothingness
that once burst into everything I see from our double wide,
our quarter porch attached by broomsticks, tarp straps,
shiny blue shingles Uncle Nick found in a dumpster
behind Long John Silvers. But the corn
tastes better if you plant it five days before
the Flower's new moon with rain from the east,
the wait worth the bounce each kernel keeps
between teeth. I've chewed enough ears to know
the pliant to firm ratio requires more patience
than preachers with jewelry habits or cousins
scraping young cobs into a pot of cubed taters
and cream, Grandpa cussing from the yard,
the latest article describing one photo
of a man and his two full moons.
Imagine what he could grow.

Uncle Nick

Materials
One grey woodshed squatting on half a yard of rusted junk metal broken by fuzzy purple thistles and nosy sunflowers. Two skinned cottontails and a six-point dripping blood from the light pole. Goats leaping between bed linens, brown pelts and t-shirts clipped to the nylon line swaying between the gutter and the corner of the shed. The house down the cut bank from the county highway. The house Grandma Winterson paid for with regret until her death at ninety-nine. The house in which Uncle Nick vacillates on a broken switch.

Objective
Primary: Foresight from hindsight, by way of relations and genetic probability. Secondary: To learn more about the variate nature of mental illness.

Background Knowledge
Uncle Nick is your father's oldest brother. He is your mother's least favorite. He is your likeness. (Especially with a beard. Strangers like to tousle both y'uns curls.) He answers the door in his tighty whities. He answers to more names than his own. He has two sons with his fourth cousin. He has two sons far removed. He is warrior and warning, all in the pitch of a high-throated scream. He is the sky in colors other than blue. He forgets to bathe.

Instruction
3 classroom hours covering:
- family dynamics
- chemical imbalance disorders
- anatomy
- choosing to stay or go

Field work involving:
- deer hunting
- field dressing
- knots
- dissection

Student Practice

Twelve Saturday hours spent in Uncle Nick's company, including hitchhiking to the flea market on the west end of town, where someone will test a rifle against the limestone and serve white beans and ham from the tailgate for their muddy truck. Minimum of one deer and one fowl must be shot in the state forest before dusk.

- Optional extra credit (good for a half-grade raise) if you photo document how to cut the midline on a squirrel using ungloved "guide fingers" with a smooth blade upturned.

- Optional extra credit (good for a bonus half day of off-campus engagement) if you produce a short video in which you feather and skin a trapped quail, open its larynx, play a few familiar chords.

Closure

Pass/fail exam. Clinical demonstration of abdominal skin removal without contamination/consternation. Certificate: Understanding Those Who Cannot Be Helped Because They Do Not Want It

Assessment

1. Pit bulls do not eat beans. T / F

2. Whiskey can be mixed safely with lithium. T / F

3. How many stomachs do sheep have? _____

4. What is the recommended daily dosage for Abilify? _____

5. Yard goats enjoy eating: (Choose any that apply.)
   a. grass
   b. chicken bones
   c. soda cans
   d. small children

6. Pigs do not perspire. T / F

7. Which type of knife works best when skinning a fawn? _____

8. Hearing voices is what type of hallucination:
   a. dietary
   b. auditory
   c. hereditary
   d. tertiary

Essay: Explain why you resemble your uncle.

Essay: How do you remove blood from sunflower seeds?

Sawyer

When Dad summoned me to the sawmill
he called me Lil Hooker, not knowing
I could unzip my mouth and spill pearls,
creek pebbles or coarse gravel depending
on who was near, was clothed or not,
whose weight I had to bear any Saturday
I risked the woods above the lake.
Gloved up, I rolled century oaks over
on the trolly, securing the dog hooks
and clamps in bark or planed sides,
before Dad summoned the track
into the saw's whir and churn.
Sawdust pelted my face, clogged
my lashes. He paid two-fifty an hour,
half what I made for hand jobs,
a quarter of my fee for signatures
I forged on permission slips.
Yesterday's field trip to the museum
ended with me triple French kissing
the most popular couple from St. Ignatius.
Chad laughed, Amy had the polaroids,
I had the receipts from the Black Friday
I drove her to the clinic in Columbus.
None of it mattered at the sawmill.
Dad guiding an oak into two by eights.
Like this, he said, holding one up,
no warp or curve, level straight.

Seizure

The bees knew
not the cost.

Grandpa held
his breath, walked

the yard, his boots unlaced,
copper aglets

kissing clover, shoving
drones off florets,

dandelions busy
with trade. He neared

the house, the yellow
oak boards free of white keel,

wing, bone
broken wishes

abandoned under cotton
thwaps. The bees

knew not to say no.
They gave their life

in defense. Grandpa
sometimes cursed, shook,

frothed or fell. I knew
not to

rub his belly
soft from work. He would

wake, and I knew
that loss

every Sunday I could
not see you

outside our vestments
hung in the dusty bureau.

I knew
it was not the same,

and I said yes
to your breath on my neck

that night. Grandpa said
the race

to the door slammed
his heart. I did

not say no to you
or the bee

climbing
his muddy cuff.

Part Time Jobs in Appalachia

I do-si-doed round another Saturday afternoon at the ass end of Goose Creek. Down bank the Orlando Mule with a Hitler tattoo and a grip I didn't resist made me listen to "Billie Jean" for the fiftieth time. I spun on my heel like I meant it from my hips like a tease, the river marooning flotsam on the boat ramp behind us. I hollered *Eeee heee!* at an octave too high to echo across the river where real vice evaded arrest with intent to distribute at the park & ride and truckers idled their rigs for lizards coming through the lot in freight shadows. Muncie Semi Guy grabbed my thigh, growled *You're getting a little too big,* picking up the scent of the new thicket below the ripped waist of my Wranglers. I took a pouty drag off his joint, dropped to my knees in his sleeper next to his blue and white cooler of Coors Light and Snickers, holding my breath when near his damp basement pits. He always wore ribbed grey tanks. He counted the black mollies I arranged on a white towel: two, five, ten until he yanked me by my curls, flinging three crisp twenties and a Lincoln tip at me faster than any silver-haired teller craving a smoke on her break. Two more sales and I returned to the ramp with my 150% of trickle up and Hawaiian Tropic, stripping to tight white Hanes and my Reds cap over my face, listening to the barge waves slap the limestone until Deputy Jenkins idled up asking *How much did you make?*

Enough for your cut and mine, Uncle.

Antidote

Dad handed me one leaf
of three torn from poison ivy
his chainsaw mangled after
it bounced off barbed wire
hidden in the sycamore bark.
I shook my head. He stared
like a hawk, wiped his face
with his undershirt. *Chew it.*
He stuffed a full trifoliate
in his mouth, shook the blade
closer to mine, flinging more
urushiol on my neck and arms.
Hurry, or   it won't   work.
I obeyed. It reminded me of lemons
Satan might enjoy. *Don't swallow,*
but I already knew that.
I wasn't new to the woods,
to doing foolish things
when no one nearby could point
or take the Lord's name
in pleasure. He watched me
wash my arms with jug water,
spat his mash on the dead grass.
A little longer. Resisting
my talent to swallow
required prayer: Dear Jesus,
you know I've suffered worse
blisters, some ghostly swelling,
howls clawing the dark, but
the choke of his chainsaw
concerns me this far
from the barn or house,

from an EpiPen, his brows too
narrow for me to stay,
to engage this superstition.
I've been chewing my cheek.
I'm not going to tell you again.
Lord, I've been tonguing the molar
that hasn't grown back.

Fourth Cousins

don't count
in French kissing

dares, horseshoes or hand grenades
we find in my great uncle's garage,

and the courthouse
clerk says we can't marry them

in this county anyway.
But how would I know

the senior track star
who shares my waxwing nest of curls

and green-shine eyes
doesn't know his confirmation name

matches my father's
middle name. Chosen, he says

from the bible
his mother locks in her nightstand.

He says she never reads it.
I read his lips

with my tongue
in the back of his pickup,

heads on our jacket pillows,
trying to pick where we want to go

if our parents find us out,

laughing when a grenade hisses

like a wet firecracker.
He says the new world order

terrifies his uncles
and silence equals safety

for now.
I remind him: mothers

always know. He squeezes
my hand, pulls

another pin.

Prosody, or an Origin Story

Dad blued my glutes with the big paddle,
the one with holes, my younger siblings
giggling in the hallway, not in the terror
ten swats intended to garner, Mom adding
I'd have to spend subsequent TV nights writing
*I will not attempt to choke my little brother
to death over rocks bombs or forts walls
while he has a machete* five thousand times
in blue ink, full cursive, every loop inspected
for closure, made to restart on any page with a mistake.
I didn't mind. I conquered my errant use of *won't*
on the 4th page. Between the lines I doodled
Psylocke's butterfly, Storm's hair pluming,
Gambit charging an Ace close to Havok's crotch,
and my favorite, Dazzler in the Gaultier cone bra,
the gold version from *Blond Ambition*. Pages piling,
I practiced my *o* and *r* sounds, "brother not bruther,"
and possible rhymes for machete, "sweaty" the first
my fingers felt, then "confetti" over Dazzler
severing the 623rd *machete* with her photon blast.
Mom said nothing about the margin art or the legal pad
of poems I started when my hand needed novel words
and fewer swoops, when I glamorized Lady Deathstrike
with her blade fingers through Wolverine's neck
under the 986th *death*, the hatched pool of blood
obscuring all but the *o* in the next *choke*. The bruises
dotting my butt greened to yellow-spotted brown.
Three of those poems earned a scholarship.
Some of them I adapted into short stories
about Mystique mourning Destiny, who saw
her death approaching like too many of my uncles.
I stowed some poems for a future collection
I'd attempt after my parents died, the 4998th sentence
beginning a new page, ample space for the last

while he has a machete to fall into the maw
of a Brood queen, her fangs piercing the *h*'s,
the birthmark on her triangular exoskull
Mom's initials, unnoticed as she flipped
the pages one last time and dropped them
into a metal bucket on the patio
with a struck match.

Oil & Ambivalence

I lost track of all their names
mumbled around glowing cigarettes,

cheeks bloated with waning chew,
tongues suffering undiagnosed dystrophies

and that alkaline taste of sooty fate.
I lost track of all their names

fake or fact on warm Friday nights
off the hilltop where Turkeyrun Lane

intersects Black Hollow, that steep curve
where one regular most often claimed

his name was Mike, just Mike who parked
his silver Ranger on the muddy shoulder,

strolling hands in pockets to the pine grove
in his trucker hat and stiff denim jacket.

I hoped we were not related. Our relations
were trouble enough that I snuck out

the half bath window after ten, traveling
nine miles memorized by starlight.

I lost track of all their names
and hated the way that Mike's fingers

tasted, coated with dirt and ash, oil
and ambivalence he pressed through

my lips onto my tongue to keep me
quiet, his gold ring scraping my incisors

as I fumbled into the jagged copper zipper
of his tarred dungarees, keeping track

of my name, my only name, never uttered,
from under my breath or my consent.

Death =

Simon beside me on the floor of Grandma's den,
Pillow Talk rolling credits, plates clanging in the kitchen—
I'm sweating inside my overalls and heavy coat,
Mom and the aunts around the euchre table.
Jon asks if I'll be valedictorian, then,
You should come to D.C. for spring break.
I count his four white hairs, zero teeth, three
bones propping his face, nine lesions not covered
by his sweatshirt. Simon flips to CNN,
where Miyazawa cradles President Bush,
Barbara lifting her napkin to catch his retch.
I'll check the dates as if I didn't know.
Mom's keys jangle in her purse—she's ready
to forget, Simon clicking through to George Michael
crooning in a big blue jacket—*It's much too late
to save myself from falling.* I unzip my coat,
Grandma appearing with a cake, 28 candles—
just allow a fragment of your life to wander free.
Everyone except Mom sings "Happy Birthday"—
Jon smiles, honks pink into a tissue he tucks in his sleeve.
Mom hugs the aunts, pats their bouffants,
the tissue teetering over the sofa. I reach, lifting—
it plops in my palm—so close I see his eyeballs
swimming under the cataracts. *Thank you,*
Simon says, taking the tissue with a dry one,
Mom's nails sinking into my shoulder, pulling me
back as the chorus stretches *and many morrrrrre.*

Detente

The Cincinnati team chanted *You're a redneck
cousin fucker* to a tune
I didn't know, chasing me
around the student union after we won

our first match. They didn't know
how much I needed the scholarship,

and they had the wrong cousin
from the bottom tip of Ohio's heart,
so lonely on the map

to them, green space without
place, names that sound
the same, hills too

close to breathe.
They had no idea

my father's holler
scorched my face and neck,

my older cousin's hand
cool from his fourth bottle, the envy

I had for their Gap jeans
and cubist sweaters,
Swatches surrealing daylight,
their hair invulnerable to wind. I smiled

under their insults, the spotlight
their derision provided, the allure
of *fucker* leaping
off their tongues,

as if they knew
what I did
about *glasnost*

and wanted to learn
which rumors about country boys
were true. We defeated them in the semifinals,

took second overall, after my teammate answered
Gorbachev instead of Chernenko. On the bus

headed home, I found a note
in my backpack, unfolded

a number beginning with 513,
a name I'd not heard
before he kissed me

under the Bobcat poster
in the restroom, whispering
I'll be at Marshall next fall too.

Dead Young Uncles

Side A – Pink Bracelet

Grandma said no makeup, closed casket,
no visitation, gossip left to the aunts
whispering after Mass about him,
and me, all the *unclean ways*
we liked to be. She said go see
for myself. Starched polyester
and his favorite *Obsession*
escaped the coffin, the navy suit
boxing his impossible waist and willow arms.
Two shiny pink threads pleated his white lips,
a double cross stitch I was unsure
could hold his secrets or mine.
I could be him, blood test pending,
Kaposi's pansies blooming
my de Kooning face, my hands
folded like an altar boy
over a similarly dull blue tie.
I could fit beside his sunken body,
could vote, survive a desert storm,
kiss another no-name man by the lake.
Grandma said we'd be the only ones
to miss him, to really know. I didn't
tell her I cut the threads and watched
his jaw fall to his lapel, a grave
without secrets, twisting
the pink nylon into a bracelet
hidden above my cuff.

August Gloria

Donnie and I placed homemade bulletins for the newly ascended in every pew, reconvened in the sacristy, sipping from the rubied cruet, chewing a few unblessed wafers like Christmas Catholics.

I'd always wanted to skip Easter for Daytona, found *the blood* too close to sour Mountain Berry Kool-Aid. Donnie licked the rim, said *it's Manischewitz*, chugged the rest. He always had the better ideas. Including the Friday night he set fire to the wire crib with his uncle's Everclear and a joint, to see if the corn would pop.

Mid-liturgy of the Eucharist, Donnie interrupted transubstantiation with the oxide alchemy of three chugged Sprites. Father Ramsey ignored our snickers, Donnie miming the lines about temptation leading us to lips drawn pale by restrained jaws, but here we were,

sweat beading our buzzcuts, unzipping our shorts under our starched vestments, gazes held across the altar, still not as naked as Jesus nailed above us, the congregation suspecting neither trespass nor spillage. Mine tasted like soap, Donnie's like lemons left out too long. *Like Granny's martini.*

In my first semester the following August, I practiced the myth of pineapples and wrote lyrics on Donnie's postcards from Kuwait, rhyming versions of *Amen* across their desert vistas.

Damn, I wish I was your lover

but you know I sucked off the basketball coach
the same day I stole that mail truck

idling behind Taco Bell, those two issues
of *Hustler* someone's dad had already unwrapped,

the pages curling with fingerprints
the feds have on file, the erections

bigger than the ones in *Playgirl*.
I have no problem admitting

there's something about home
I usually avoid. Houses

require too much work. Yards belong
to dandelions and sycamore saplings.

See also siblings, mothers, kids, kittens, pups,
another man's last name in my fantasy. Why pretend

I govern more than my thoughts
and cock? After the deputies made me

apologize to the mailman, I used three books
of matches from Cyndee's

to change my prints
from curved lines to keloid plains

seers say *Look like a short life
lived well*, and you said *Feels good*

when you do that, but when I close my eyes

I feel pressure behind my molars,

a cold trail and sulfur lingering,
gritting the air

like the matches
pressed between my fingertips.

Dead Young Uncles

Side B – Good to Be Seen

Both gravediggers
lost grip, wet

ropes coiling
atop Jon's coffin

bobbing like wreckage
in the hole. I couldn't

hear my mom
or the priest,

his thin lips
like worms surfaced

by the rain, searching
for perpetual light

and the benefits of prayer
for the dead. Someone

behind me shouted *Amen*.
The priest closed his missal.

Our pickup procession
flying purple flags

crawled to Grandma's
corner two-story, the sun

backlighting the yard.
I saw more

empty beer cans
than mourners

grazing deli platters
and Jon's friend Henri

in neck-to-knee black
linen, cross-legged

and regal in a chair
by the fence, smiling

like 1980,
like he wasn't

the only one left.
He waved

a slow Evita pivot,
his tambourine

of bracelets
ignoring mumbles

from cousins
who wouldn't look

when he hugged me,
his arms unspooling

like nylon hem,
his torso caved

with welcome
and lost mass.

I held him
and inhaled. *That's Yves*

Rocher, honey. Two
snaps and I kissed

his cheek. *It's good
to see you, uncle.*

He spun on his heel,
winking. *Cause it's good*

to be seen–click clacking
down the sidewalk

smiling, his teeth
yellow as box cake.

Strange Orange

Thank you for breaking
into my locker to kick
off sophomore year, dumping

its contents onto my lap in
homeroom, lamenting the lack
of revelation like an accusation, as if

I'd do that to you. Thank you
for laughing, I laughed too, the only one
who knew as you strutted away,

your buddies braying, slapping
your back, swaying to a chorus of *Ha ha
homo queer*. They didn't know

you were one too and I learned
from my grandfather's pet
crow how missing things are

thesauruses of secrets you thought
you were keeping until that night, years
later, on the sofa in your cousin's trailer,

you had returned from Iraq with more
muscles than words, more red than blue
in your eyes squeezed shut as I rubbed

the lumps around your pale scalp,
laughing about your once pretty black curls
that wooed all the girls. Thank you

for laughing too, unbuttoning your shirt,
my tongue through your lips,
my fingers climbing your ribs, skipping

your lost nipple. I traced the hard pink
scar across your abdomen, *It's ok*,
ending with a knot of dead flesh

where your navel used to be
when your tears were clear,
not this strange, luminescent orange.

Dress Nice and Smell Good

Dad stomped off the porch,
my letters from Northwestern
and Ohio State in his fist. I listened

to Aunt Janice say *that furrow
separating my eyebrows is a sure sign
of Satan's work.* She knew

about me, about men, my business
inked above rest stop urinals. She reached
in her cooler, popped another Dew.

*You gotta go. Even if he won't co-sign,
get to the city. Go to community college.
Find weird boys who dress nice and smell good*

*and like to dance and drink wine and say hello
to the devil and strangers the same.*
The farm taught me time devils itself,

like the oaks adding thinner rings
before cicada years, Dad circling the yard,
thumping nephews who cussed or stomped

Mom's tulips. Like the stars of any season
above the loblollies, the men against them
always itching. *Unclench, baby,* Janice circled

her flush face with her seven-ringed hand,
*because stress leads to wrinkles and wrinkles
lead to lonely and lonely seasons your heart*

*with a rub no ice cream or whiskey can cure.
Speaking of which.* She emptied her flask

into her Dew, pulled an envelope

from her purse. *For you.* Two Benjamins, handwritten directions to a Super 8 outside Columbus, a blank check.

To be continued.

Whine

(Desire Psalm, 19:3)

My nasal whine's so high it reaches heaven,
chromosomes and bodily fluids

ignited by bullies and nurture,
my vocal fry a ruin

the devil calls swagger.
But I see how many men

fear what they can't keep
under thumb, what submission means

if flipped, their privilege
not a granite mountain,

but a worn pebble skipping the lake
we gather near at dusk,

threading reeds and thighs,
my squeak unleashed

like a frog's tongue, sticky
and quick near their ear,

their loose gasps, their shudders
crowned with touch-me-nots

when I touch them,
we break their secret

joy under my thumb,
pressed between their lips,

a ruin I call
from their bellies

pressed into the ground,
their pitch so high

gnats and bats scatter and all
I hear is *harder,   yes,   please.*

Glasnost

Unless you count the silver cock ring
the preacher's son slipped on
when I asked if he could be mine—

I never came out, not officially.

I promised I'd not chosen from
my four offers for full rides
in other states, and he helped me

edit my commencement speech
above his comforter, knowing

he was between the Buckeyes
and Bobcats, but not the idea of us—

I told my family, over Easter break,
I'd changed my mind about Ohio,

the new world order Uncle Ricky insisted
we were about to enter. The Soviets,
he claimed, were right

to build the wall. To keep the past
safe from the future.

So was I.

Twang

From tongue's tip, I fling every *ing* off
tempo, picking up speed, running on

the holler version of holy rolling
cousins identified by pink bumps,

red glands, the occasional chancre
flattening everything good. It's twang

at the dinner table, diss communicating.
Twang on the radio, strumming

joy, bluegrass played backward,
your yellow lab jumping back in

your suddenly running pickup.
Twang in barn sale cattle calls, math

so fast in your head no one notices
the price of hay or the dead.

                Chase that rabbit / Chase that squirrel
                Chase that pretty boy / Round the world.

The uncles and oaks twang too,
baring their veiny white bellies

to the Atlantic churning dark blue,
furious with premonitions of Andrew.

The college guys next door challenge
us to volleyball and jello shots

in apple, mango or mountain breeze.
They sound like me rooted in red clay,

but more bass, and I note the stain,
menace the vodka sharpens every time

their spikes dent the sand. The tallest
tells me and my aunts he attends Auburn,

studying law. His stare says he knows
how to break it.

        Every man dances / Every man swings
        Every man does / The same damned thing

Under the deck at dusk, my tongue twists
Auburn Senior's, his chest hairy, wide

and ripe with sweat and sand, Old Spice
and Dr. Pepper, my belly's swoon

stirred by his Tuscaloosa croon.
Indigo climbs the line of sea sky,

my feet in his lap, my pinky tracing
the vascular map of his hand, knowing

there was no going back. He says *It's cute
how you say y'uns instead of y'all,*

and I smile like my dead uncles said to
when a man talks nice. *Don't tell*

anyone. He promises he'll call. I don't
even ask his name. I have to go.

        Boys to the left / Men to the right
        He never called, but I / do-si-doed all night

Holler Psalm 6:02

Bless your femurs of iron ore. Grandma said *hers too* were once sturdy in winter ice, stern against summer's august core. May they steel you through Manhattan canyons. Bless your flinty olecranon, sparking every time your uncle shattered empty bottles against it, your silica ulna a shield your father envied behind his silent concessions. He was all talc, clavicles slack under his brother's weighty rage. Bless your phosphate kneecaps. Bless your graphite nails and feldspar fingers graphing strangers in the dark without leaving a mark. May they always pleasure the world. Bless the quartz click clack of your nails on your manual typewriter, the poems you wrote when your mother refused to play along, called herself coal, absorbing any light she could, stowing it in her marrow of slick mud and thick silt, a sinking you learned as love. May your chalk wrist continue saying otherwise, swinging below the line, belts, drawing stall art, new memes and last names, a life in the margins. Bless the shale storing your past behind your sternum. Bless the dolomite sockets of your diamond eyes, set to stun straight on or from the side, depending on the fella, day and time. Bless your gypsum lips. You know why.

Always August

Every oak slouching, alfalfa on the wind.
Yellow-pitted t-shirts on the pickup seat.
I still have dirt between my teeth
In a previous version of our living room
Dad says, *the lazy are damned.* Mom nods.
My tongue like a snow drift,
But what can I say? I'm not dying
In this swelter even cardinals flee.
Sweat slinks down my neck.
Sweat from men who ask my name
And undress like it's always August.
Maybe it's my disdain for dirt
Cold January against my cheek,
The devil shaking his dandruff
Over parked cars, naked oaks, gravel
Peppering my footprints. Maybe
I just understand August. Its drought
Of good choices. Last night,
The ivies curled and left no blisters.
Cattle kept to the shade, tails raising
Dust against flies. The hayfield
Perfumed my arms. Dad asks *Does it
make you happy?* The hills wait.
Limestone ruddies. Days shorten.
I reach into the burn barrel. *I don't know,*
Behind me, a match striking. *I might
be damned.* More men. I turn
Into September.

Notes

"Country Queer:" In the last preglacial era, the Teays River flowed north out of the current Ohio River basin. Sections of the Teays still exist in West Virginia as the New River and the Kanawha River.

"Reading Is Fundamental:" The title is a nod to the seminal Jennie Livingston documentary *Paris Is Burning*. The poem interpolates lyrics from several songs on *diana*, the 1980 hit album from the legendary Diana Ross. "claws of metal eagles" refers to Operation Eagle Claw, the failed 1980 military operation to rescue hostages from the US embassy in Tehran, Iran.

"Cento for 1985:" This cento uses lyrics from and/or references numerous hit and theme songs, films, and television shows from late 1984 and 1985. Included songs and shows/films include: *Cheers, Raspberry Beret, One More Night, Crazy for You, Never Surrender, Take Me With You, Every Time You Go Away, Everybody Wants to Rule the World, Shout, Take On Me, Into the Groove, Would I Lie to You, Careless Whisper, Easy Lover, Growing Pains, How Will I Know, You Belong to the Night, V, Dynasty, Golden Girls, We Don't Need Another Hero, Back to the Future, Boys of Summer, Walking on Sunshine, Alive and Kicking,* and *Fortress Around My Heart*.

"Silence = Death:" Rock Hudson, one of the biggest stars of Hollywood's studio era, died of AIDS-related causes in October 1985, just weeks after admitting he was ill with the virus. His death elevated awareness and action related to the virus.

"First Cousins:" Reimagines a scene from Walt Whitman's "I Sing the Body Electric."

"Cottonmouth:" The Star Wars in this poem refers to the nickname for

President Ronald Reagan's Strategic Defense Initiative. His idea was to create a system of missile (and potentially satellite) defenses that would counter any nuclear attack, potentially ending the idea of mutually assured destruction.

"Calliphora Vomitoria:" Calliphora vomitoria, the blue bottle fly, is a species of blow fly known for laying eggs in fresh corpses.

"Damned Spots:" toils over a cauldron filled with Shakespeare's *Macbeth*, Madonna and George Michael at their creative nadirs, and evangelical villains of the 1980s.

"Common Source Minerals in the Bottom Tip of Ohio's Heart:" Borrows its form from a type of geological chart comparing layers of rock by age and type.

The pawpaw tree and its fruit highlighted in "Pawpaw" are native Appalachia flora. An edible fruit with which some old timers used to make questionable desserts, the seeds (as well as the leaves and bark) contain a dangerous neurotoxin. We called them "hillbilly avocados" growing up. They do not taste or smell like avocados.

"They Say Men Are Always About Looks:" At the time of her introduction in the early 1980s, the X-Men character Rogue possesses the mutant power to temporarily borrow the powers of whomever she touches. However, she also absorbs their mind, memories, lifeforce and personality traits. Which is why her uniforms covered her head-to-toe.

A palindrome as a fable, "My Villain Origin Story" borrows several turns of phrase from Madonna's international hit song from 1990, *Vogue*.

"To August:" This poem pays modern homage to Keats's "Ode to a Grecian Urn" and partakes of the world in August of 1990, when Iraq invaded Kuwait. The Skyline Drive is a scenic, mountain top route through the Blue Ridge Mountains. Arthur Kent was a CNN war reporter who became a subject of swoon for many viewers. Active denial systems were experimental microwave weapons tested during Desert Storm.

"Uncle Nick:" This poem mimics the form of a teacher's lesson plan.

"Antidote:" My grandmother swore that you could prevent poison ivy, before or after exposure, by chewing a leaf of the plant to cud.

"Fourth Cousins:" When completing the sacrament of confirmation, many young Catholic are encouraged to take an additional confirmation name from either an ancestor or Biblical hero.

"Death =:" references *Don't Let the Sun Go Down on Me*, a song written by Elton John and Bernie Taupin, performed live by George Michael and Elton John in 1991 during Michael's *Cover to Cover* tour. The duet hit #1 on the Billboard Hot 100 in February 1992.

"Detente:" This poem mentions glasnost, the policy of social and political openness promoted by Mikhail Gorbachev of the former Soviet Union. Gorbachev and Konstantin Chernenko were Soviet leaders in the 1980s.

"Damn I wish I was your lover:" The title comes from the 1992 hit by Sophie B. Hawkins, *Damn, I Wish I Was Your Lover*, from her debut album *Tongues and Tails*.

"Prosody, or an Origin Story:" This poem mentions several X-Men characters and plot beats popular during the Outback era of *Uncanny X-Men*, as written and drawn by Chris Claremont and Marc Silvestri. Gambit debuted near the end of this era, and the Brood were a parasitic alien species who'd long been enemies of the X-Men.

"Dress Nice and Smell Good:" In areas of the US Midwest where the Brood X cicada are common, many trees experience smaller rings not just from droughts, but from the two to three years preceding the Brood X rising, because the growing larvae feast on the soil and roots of trees before their 17 year emergence.

"Twang:" This poem interpolates calls from the square dance *Chase the Rabbit*. It also mentions Hurricane Andrew, a 1992 category 5 storm that devastated large parts of Florida and the southeastern US coast.

Acknowledgements

Many thanks to the following journals in which these poems (or earlier versions of them) appeared:

"The New Math" – *Juked*

"Country Queer" and "Red Spots in the Snow" – *apt*

"Let Us Pray" and "B" – *I Thought I Heard a Cardinal Sing: Ohio's Appalachian Voices*

"Reading Is Fundamental" – *Grist Online*

"Hayfield Prayer" – *POETRY*

"Be a Good Boy" and "Strange Orange" – *Homology Lit*

"Cottonmouth – *Kettle Blue Review*

"Plague" and "Flower Moon: – *Emerge Poetry Journal*

"Second Cousins" – *Five South*

"Will / Inherit" – *Vagabond City Lit* and *Dead Uncles*

"Common Source Minerals in the Bottom Tip of Ohio's Heart" – *Gordon Square Review*

"Redneck Arithmetic" and "Uncle Nick" – *DIAGRAM*

"Bullies" – *Cutbank Literary Journal*

"August Aubade" – *Rappahannock Review*

"They Say Men Are All About Looks" – *Lunch Ticket*

"A Lisp" and "Holler Psalm 6:02" – *Pithead Chapel*

"August Serenade" – *Ghost City Review*

"Seizure" – *Thrush*

"Part Time Jobs in Appalachia" – *Dead Uncles*

"Antidote" – *The Florida Review*

"Prosody, or an Origin Story" – *Variant Literature*

"Oil & Ambivalence" – *Impossible Archetype*

"Dead Young Uncles: Side A - Pink Bracelet" – *HIV Here & Now Daily Poem Series*

"Whine" – *Cherry Tree*

Thank you to the farm, my family, my grandparents especially, public schools, and all the friends and fellow writers who helped me shape this collection.

Special shoutout to Todd Dillard and Sandra Beasley for all their guidance.

About the Author

Hailing from the farmland valleys of the west Appalachian foothills, Ben Kline (he/him) lives in Cincinnati, Ohio. A poet, library professional, storyteller, and renowned exaggerator, Ben is the author of the chapbooks *Sagittarius A** and *Dead Uncles*, as well as the collections *It Was Never Supposed to Be* (Variant Literature) and *Stiff Wrist* (fourteen poems.) His work has appeared in *Poet Lore, Copper Nickel, Florida Review, Southeast Review, DIAGRAM, Poetry,* and other publications.

Photo credit: Harold Daniels

www.ingramcontent.com/pod-product-compliance
Lightning Source LLC
Chambersburg PA
CBHW030748170426
43196CB00026BA/997